the hot and spicy book

charmaine solomon

HAMLYN

Notes

Convert cup measures to metric or
imperial measures where necessary.
Use one set of measurements only and
not a mixture. Standard level spoon
measurements are used in all recipes.
Eggs should be size 3 unless otherwise stated.
Milk should be full fat unless otherwise stated.
Pepper should be freshly milled unless
otherwise stated.
Fresh herbs should be used unless
otherwise stated. If unavailable use dried herbs as
an alternative but halve the quantities stated.
For ease of reference:
Capsicum = Pepper
Eggplant = Aubergine
Zucchini = Courgette

First published in Great Britain in 1996 by Hamlyn,
an imprint of Reed Consumer Books Limited
Michelin House, 81 Fulham Road,
London SW3 6RB
and Auckland, Melbourne,
Singapore and Toronto

Published 1995 by Mandarin
a part of Reed Books Australia
22 Salmon Street, Port Melbourne
Victoria 3207
a division of Reed International Books
Australia Pty Limited

First published in 1993 by Hamlyn Australia as part
of Charmaine Solomon's Asian Cooking Library.

Designed by Guy Mirabella
Photographs by Michael Cook
Styling by Margaret Alcock
Food cooked by Nina Harris, Jill Pavey
China: Villeroy & Boch, Australia Pty Ltd

ISBN for UK edition 0 600 59026 7
ISBN for Australian edition 1 86330 441 x

A CIP catalogue for this book is available from the
British Library
Produced by Mandarin Offset
Printed and bound in Hong Kong

1. Cookery (Curry). 2. Spices 3. Cookery, Oriental.
4. Cookery, India. I. Solomon, Charmaine, Curried
and Spiced. II. Solomon, Charmaine. Classic Indian
cooking. III. Title. IV. Title: Curried and Spiced. V.
Title: Classic Indian Cooking.

A Metric/Imperial guide to Australian solid and liquid measures

Liquid Measures

Australian	Metric	Imperial
1 cup	250 ml	8 fl oz
½ cup	125 ml	4 fl oz
⅓ cup	75 ml	3 fl oz

Solid Measures

Australian	Metric	Imperial
1 cup	300 g	10 oz
½ cup	150 g	5 oz
⅓ cup	125 g	4 oz

Liquid Measures/Teaspoons/Tablespoons

A teaspoon holds approximately 5 ml in both
Australia and Britain. The British standard tablespoon
holds 15 ml, whilst the Australian holds 20ml.

Australian	British
1 teaspoon	1 teaspoon
1 tablespoon	1 tablespoon
2 tablespoons	2 tablespoons
3 ½ tablespoons	3 tablespoons
4 tablespoons	3 ½ tablespoons

contents

In many parts of Asia the chief sources of protein are oceans, rivers, ponds and streams that provide fish, crustaceans, molluscs and other edible sea creatures. The long coastlines with their rich harvest inspire cooks to find varied ways of preparing fresh seafood, and the recipes that follow focus on this. However, Asians are equally resourceful in preserving the catch, which explains why dried and salted fish, fish sauce, shrimp paste and dried shrimp are so much part of the everyday diet, doubling as seasoning and protein component.

thai
red curry of fish

serves 4-5

750 g (1 1/2 lb) steaks or fillets of
  firm white fish
1 teaspoon turmeric
  salt
4 tablespoons peanut oil
3 tablespoons Thai Red Curry
  Paste (see p. 88)
4 shallots, finely chopped finely
  grated rind of 1 lime

1 cup canned coconut milk
4 kaffir lime leaves
8 small red or green chillies
2 tablespoons fish sauce
1 tablespoon palm sugar
  juice of 1 lime or half
  lemon
20 fresh basil leaves

Rub fish with turmeric and salt and fry lightly in hot oil. In oil remaining in wok fry Red Curry Paste and shallots, stirring constantly, until fragrant. Add grated lime rind, coconut milk, 1 cup water, lime leaves, whole chillies, fish sauce and sugar. Simmer uncovered for 10 minutes.

Add fish steaks and continue simmering for a further 10 minutes. Stir in lime juice and basil leaves and serve at once with steamed rice and a vegetable dish, such as Bean Sayur (see p. 60).

bengal fish curry

If you are able to buy fresh curry leaves and pandan leaves the flavour of this curry will be much better. These are becoming increasingly common in Asian shops.

serves 4

500 g (1 lb) fish fillets
salt to taste
2 teaspoons ground turmeric
4 dried red chillies, seeded
1 teaspoon chopped fresh ginger
1 cup plain yoghurt, beaten until
smooth
2 tablespoons mustard oil or
vegetable oil
2 tablespoons ghee

2 bay leaves
2 cassia leaves, optional
1 onion, sliced thinly
2 fresh green chillies, split in
halves lengthwise
1 teaspoon Garam Masala
(see p. 84)
2 tablespoons chopped coriander
leaves

Cut fish fillets into large serving pieces and rub with salt and turmeric. Soak dried chillies in a little boiling water for 15 minutes, then place in a blender with ginger and process to a fine paste, gradually adding yoghurt. Pour over fish and marinate for 10 minutes.

Heat oil and ghee in a saucepan. Add bay and cassia leaves, onion and fresh chillies and fry until onion starts to brown. Stir in fish and all marinade and sprinkle with Garam Masala. Cover and cook over low heat for 10 minutes. Serve sprinkled with coriander leaves and accompanied by rice.

Note   Cassia leaves are sold as 'tej pattar' in Indian shops.

ri lankan fish curry with tamarind

serves 4

4 cutlets of jewfish, Spanish
   mackerel or cod
turmeric
salt and freshly ground
   black pepper
oil for frying
2 sprigs fresh curry leaves or
   20 dried
2 large onions, finely chopped
1 teaspoon fenugreek seeds

2 teaspoons finely chopped garlic
2 teaspoons finely grated
   fresh ginger
1 small stick cinnamon
   strip of fresh, frozen or dried
   pandan leaf
2 tablespoons Ceylon Curry
   Powder (see p. 82)
1 tablespoon dried tamarind pulp
1 cup canned coconut milk

Rub cutlets with turmeric, salt and pepper. In a large pan heat 3 tablespoons oil and on low heat fry curry leaves, onions, fenugreek seeds, garlic, ginger, cinnamon and pandan leaf until onions are soft and golden. Add curry powder and fry for 2 minutes, stirring.

Soak tamarind pulp in $1/2$ cup hot water and when cool squeeze to dissolve pulp. Strain, discarding seeds and fibres. Add to pan. Stir in coconut milk mixed with $1/2$ cup water and simmer, uncovered, until sauce thickens.

Put in fish steaks and spoon sauce over. Simmer for about 10 minutes. Serve hot with rice and vegetables.

hot
prawn curry

serves 6

1 kg (2 lb) raw prawns
6 large, dried red chillies
1 large onion, chopped
3 cloves garlic, chopped
1 tablespoon chopped fresh ginger
4 tablespoons oil
2 sprigs fresh curry leaves

1 teaspoon ground turmeric
2 teaspoons ground coriander
1 teaspoon ground cummin
1 teaspoon paprika
salt to taste
1$^1/_4$ cups canned coconut milk
lime or lemon juice to taste

Remove heads and devein prawns, leaving legs and body shells intact, rinse with cold water and drain. Soak chillies in hot water for 5 minutes. (If you want a milder curry, break off stem ends of chillies, shake out and discard seeds.) Put soaked chillies into a blender or food processor with onion, garlic and ginger and purée.

Heat oil in a heavy saucepan and gently fry curry leaves for 10 seconds, then stir in puréed mixture. Fry, stirring constantly, for about 5 minutes, or until the mixture gives off an aromatic smell and oil starts to separate out from edges. Stir in ground spices and paprika and fry for 1 minute more. Add prawns and stir until they change colour. Add salt and coconut milk with 1 cup water. Stir and simmer, uncovered, for 10 minutes. Remove from heat and add lime or lemon juice to taste. Serve with rice.

chilli prawns

For a dish that is so simple to make, the results are outstandingly tasty. If you are not really into hot flavours, use a sweet chilli sauce and hold back on the fresh chillies.

serves 4

500 g (1 lb) large, raw prawns
$^1/_4$ cup peanut oil
$^1/_2$ cup chopped spring onions
2 teaspoons finely grated
  fresh ginger
2 teaspoons crushed garlic
2 or 3 red chillies, finely chopped

$^1/_4$ cup chilli sauce
$^1/_4$ cup tomato ketchup
1 tablespoon sugar
1 tablespoon light
  soy sauce
salt to taste

Shell and devein prawns, leaving only the tail on. In a wok, heat oil and fry spring onions, ginger, garlic and chillies, stirring, until fragrant. Add chilli sauce and tomato ketchup, sugar, soy sauce and salt, stirring to dissolve sugar. Add prawns and toss in mixture until well coated and cooked through. Serve with steamed white rice.

masala king prawns

serves 4-6

750 g (1¹/₂ lb) raw king prawns
8 large dried red chillies
2 teaspoons chopped fresh ginger
2 cloves garlic, chopped
¹/₂ teaspoon ground cinnamon
¹/₄ teaspoon ground cloves
1 teaspoon ground cummin
¹/₂ teaspoon ground turmeric
ground black pepper to taste

¹/₄ cup red wine vinegar
¹/₃ cup oil
2 medium onions, sliced finely
1 green capsicum, sliced
3 ripe tomatoes, peeled and
chopped
2 tablespoons lime or lemon juice
salt to taste

Wash and drain prawns, but do not shell. Soak chillies in hot water for 5 minutes. Drain chillies, reserving soaking water. Put ginger, garlic, chillies and a little of soaking water into a blender or food processor and blend until smooth. Add spices and vinegar and mix.

Heat oil in a heavy-based saucepan and fry onions and capsicum, stirring frequently, until soft. Add prawns and fry over high heat, turning them over, just until they change colour. Stir in blended mixture and fry, stirring, for about 5 minutes. Add tomatoes, lime juice and salt, simmering, covered, for 10 minutes. Serve with rice.

crab curry

This curry is best made with live crabs. My method for coping with these nippy monsters is to let them go quietly to sleep in the freezer first. Whenever we had this in Sri Lanka, a wooden board and heavy hammer were brought to the table and each diner cracked the claws with a well placed blow while others at the table hid behind their napkins in case of flying curry! Serve only with rice, no other curries or accompaniments, because the flavour is so superb it deserves to be appreciated on its own. Besides, you are so busy picking meat from the crabs there is just no time to concentrate on anything else.

serves 4-6

2 large crabs
3 medium onions, chopped finely
6 cloves garlic, chopped finely
2 teaspoons finely grated
  fresh ginger
1/2 teaspoon fenugreek seeds
  sprig of curry leaves
8 cm (3 inch) stick cinnamon

1 teaspoon chilli powder
1 teaspoon ground turmeric
2 teaspoons salt or to taste
3 1/2 cups canned coconut milk
2 tablespoons desiccated coconut
1 tablespoon ground rice
1/4 cup lime or lemon juice

Remove carapace, the hard top shell, from crabs and discard 'feathers' found underneath.

Divide each crab into 4 sections: break each body in half, leaving legs attached, but detach large claws from body.

Put onion, garlic, ginger, fenugreek, curry leaves, cinnamon, chilli, turmeric, salt and 1 1/2

cups of the coconut milk mixed with 2 1/2 cups water into a large saucepan. Cover and simmer gently for 30 minutes. Add crabs. Make sure pieces of crab are submerged in sauce while cooking, otherwise simmer half the pieces at a time.

If using raw crabs cook for 20 minutes, but cooked crabs should be simmered for only

8 minutes.

Toast desiccated coconut and ground rice separately in a dry frying pan over medium heat,

stirring constantly, until each is golden brown—watch that they don't burn. Transfer to a blender container and add 1 cup of coconut milk. Blend for 1 minute on high speed, then stir into curry with lime or lemon juice. Rinse blender with remaining cup of coconut milk and stir in. Simmer uncovered for 10 minutes more. Serve with plain boiled rice.

thai
stuffed mussels

serves 4

500 g (1 lb) mussels
185 g (6 oz) minced pork
3 teaspoons Thai Red Curry Paste
  (see p. 88)
  grated rind of 1/2 lime
2 tablespoons finely chopped
  spring onions

2 teaspoons cornflour
3 teaspoons fish sauce
1 teaspoon palm sugar
1 egg white
  red chillies
  fresh coriander leaves

Scrub mussels with a stiff brush and beard them by tugging

brown fibres near hinge of shell. Discard mussels that

are not tightly shut. Place on a rack and steam just

until shells open. Remove from heat and remove

empty half of shell from each mussel.

Combine pork, Thai Red Curry Paste, rind, spring onions,

cornflour, fish sauce, palm sugar and egg white.

Spread a teaspoon of mixture over each mussel. Place

shreds of chilli and small coriander leaves on each and

arrange once again in steamer. Steam for 15 minutes.

hot
-sour prawn soup

serves 6

500 g (1 lb) small to medium
   raw prawns
1 tablespoon oil
1 teaspoon salt
2 or 3 stems fresh lemon grass,
   thinly sliced or thinly peeled
   rind of 1 lemon
4 slices greater galangal, fresh,
   brined or frozen

4 fresh or frozen kaffir lime leaves
4 fresh red chillies
3 teaspoons chopped garlic
1 tablespoon palm sugar
2 tablespoons fish sauce
$^1/_4$ cup lime juice or more to taste
$^1/_4$ cup chopped fresh
   coriander leaves
$^1/_4$ cup sliced spring onions

Shell and devein prawns, saving heads and shells for making stock. Heat oil in a saucepan and fry heads and shells until they turn red. Add 2 litres water, salt, lemon grass, galangal, lime leaves, 3 of the chillies and garlic. Cover and simmer for 20 minutes, then strain stock.

Rinse saucepan and return stock. Add prawns and simmer for a few minutes, just until they turn opaque and curl. Add palm sugar, fish sauce and lime juice to taste, remove from heat and serve sprinkled with remaining chilli finely sliced, coriander and spring onions.

Where you shop can determine what certain ingredients are called. To avoid confusion when using this book and buying poultry, here is a short explanation.

Thigh fillets are the thigh meat with skin and bone removed. Thigh cutlets are the thigh joint with skin and bone intact. Chicken thighs are thigh cutlets with a large bit of backbone attached. Chicken soup pieces are usually necks, backs, carcases (with breast fillets removed) and some offcuts of drumsticks if you're lucky. The latter are cheap and ideal for making stock.

To cut chicken into curry pieces means jointing the chicken and then cutting through the joints to make smaller pieces so that spices can penetrate and flavour the meat. A breast should be halved, then each half cut into 3. Thighs and drumsticks should be cut into 2 pieces each. (In Chinese dishes, however, they are cut into 5, not separating them at the joint but chopping either side of the joint and then 2 more cuts on each side. Use a heavy, sharp Chinese cleaver for this sort of chopping through the bone, or you will ruin your best knives.)

Here then is poultry the Asian way—in curries, tangy soups, tantalising stir-fries and spicy braised dishes.

thai
chicken and galangal soup

There are many flavours in this spicy soup, but the predominant one is galangal, also known as Thai ginger.

serves 6

1 kg (2 lb) chicken soup pieces
2 cups canned coconut milk
$^1/_2$ teaspoon whole black peppercorns
6 slices galangal, fresh or in brine
3 stems lemon grass, finely sliced
4 fresh coriander roots,
    finely chopped
4 fresh green chillies

$1^1/_2$ teaspoons salt or to taste
6 kaffir lime leaves
1–2 tablespoons fish sauce
$^1/_3$ cup strained lime juice
$^1/_2$ cup chopped fresh
    coriander leaves
500 g (1 lb) chicken thighs,
    skin removed

Put chicken soup pieces in a large saucepan with 2 litres water, 1 cup coconut milk and all ingredients except lime juice, coriander leaves and chicken thighs. Bring to the boil and simmer for 1 hour, strain and put thighs in liquid to cook for a further 35 minutes, returning lime leaves and galangal. Dice chicken meat and return to soup with remaining coconut milk, lime juice and coriander. Serve hot.

indonesian
egg sambal

Serve with rice or as an exciting filling for sandwiches.

serves 4-6

4 eggs
3 tablespoons peanut oil
1 onion, finely chopped
1 teaspoon crushed garlic
$^1/_2$ teaspoon dried shrimp paste
1 tablespoon sambal ulek or
    chopped red chillies
1 teaspoon finely chopped
    galangal, fresh or bottled

6 candlenuts or macadamias,
    finely grated or pounded
2 teaspoons palm sugar
$^1/_2$ cup canned coconut milk
    salt to taste
2 tablespoons lime or lemon juice

Have eggs at room temperature or gently warm them in tepid water before cooking them.

Stir for the first few minutes so yolks are centred, then simmer for 8 minutes. Cool in a bowl of cold water. Shell eggs and halve lengthways.

Heat oil and fry onion and garlic until onion is soft and golden. Add shrimp paste, sambal, galangal and candlenuts and fry, stirring, until fragrant. Add palm sugar, coconut milk, salt and lime juice and simmer, stirring frequently, until oil shines on surface. Put in eggs, spooning sauce over.

sri lankan chicken curry

serves 4-6

3 tablespoons ghee or oil
10 curry leaves
2 large onions, chopped finely
5 cloves garlic, chopped finely
2 teaspoons finely grated fresh
   ginger
2 tablespoons Ceylon Curry
   Powder (see p. 82)
2 teaspoons salt

2 tablespoons vinegar
1.5 kg (3 lb) roasting chicken,
   jointed
2 ripe tomatoes, peeled
   and chopped
6 cardamom pods, bruised
1 stick cinnamon
1 stalk lemon grass, bruised
1 cup canned coconut milk

Heat ghee and fry curry leaves until they start to brown. Add onions, garlic and ginger and fry over low heat until onions are soft and golden, stirring frequently. Stir in Ceylon Curry Powder, salt and vinegar. Add chicken pieces and cook over medium heat, turning until thoroughly coated. Add tomatoes, whole spices and lemon grass and cook, covered, over low heat for 40 minutes or until tender. Stir in coconut milk and heat through. Serve with rice and accompaniments.

chicken
with chilli radish

serves 4

500 g chicken thigh fillets
$^1/_2$ teaspoon salt
$^1/_2$ teaspoon five spice powder
3 tablespoons peanut oil
2 teaspoons finely grated ginger
1 teaspoon finely chopped garlic
2 tablespoons preserved
   hot radish

2 tablespoons soy sauce
2 tablespoons dry sherry
$^1/_4$ cup chicken stock
$1^1/_2$ teaspoons cornflour
1 teaspoon sesame oil

Cut chicken fillets into bite-sized squares and rub over with salt and five spice powder.

Heat oil in a wok and gently fry ginger and garlic for 30 seconds, then add hot radish and fry for a further 10 seconds before adding chicken and stir-frying on high heat until colour changes.

Add soy sauce, sherry and stock and bring to the boil. Cover and simmer for 3 minutes.

Mix cornflour with a little cold water and stir into sauce until it boils and thickens. Sprinkle sesame oil over and toss well. Serve with steamed rice.

thai
chicken curry with basil

serves 6

500 g (1 lb) chicken thigh fillets
500 g (1 lb) sugar snap peas
3 tablespoons peanut oil
3 tablespoons Thai Red Curry
   Paste (see p. 88)
finely grated rind of 1 lime

5 kaffir lime leaves
2 tablespoons fish sauce
1$^1/_2$ cups canned coconut milk
1 tablespoon palm sugar
20 fresh lemon basil or sweet
   basil leaves

Cut chicken into bite-sized pieces and remove strings from pea pods. Heat oil in a wok and fry Red Curry Paste over low heat, stirring, until fragrant—about 5 minutes. Add chicken and fry until pieces are coated with paste. Add lime rind, lime leaves, fish sauce, coconut milk plus 1 cup water and simmer for 10 minutes, uncovered.

Drop peas into lightly salted boiling water for 1 minute. Do not overcook. Lift out with slotted spoon and simmer with chicken for a minute or so. Stir in palm sugar. Remove from heat, add basil leaves. Serve with rice.

braised mandarin chicken

500 g (1 lb) chicken Maryland
2 mandarins
2 tablespoons dry sherry
2 tablespoons dark soy sauce
2 teaspoons sugar
2 teaspoons green peppercorns
  in brine

2 tablespoons peanut oil
2 teaspoons finely chopped
  fresh ginger
3 or 4 dried red chillies, whole
3 or 4 fresh hot chillies, sliced
1/2 cup spring onions, sliced
1 teaspoon sesame oil

Cut chicken thighs and drumsticks into 4 or 5 pieces each using a heavy cleaver and
chopping straight through bones. Do not separate at joint, but cut on either side of it.

Squeeze juice from 1 mandarin, combine with sherry, soy sauce and sugar. Crush green
peppercorns and mix in. Scoop out pith from mandarin halves and cut rind into fine shreds. Wrap in
plastic to prevent drying out.

Heat a wok, add peanut oil and when hot fry ginger, dried chillies, fresh chillies and
mandarin rind for about 10 seconds. Add chicken pieces and fry on high heat, tossing and pressing
against sides of wok, until no longer pink. Add combined liquid ingredients, cover and simmer for 20
to 30 minutes until chicken is tender. Turn pieces in sauce now and then so they are evenly coloured.
Meanwhile, peel and segment remaining mandarin.

Add spring onions and cook on high heat, uncovered, until sauce reduces. Sprinkle with
sesame oil and garnish with mandarin segments. Serve with steamed rice.

madras chicken curry

This is typical of south Indian curries—rather fiery due to the amount of chilli! You can use less chilli powder and still have a delicious curry with a rich coconut milk sauce.

serves 6

1 x 1.5 kg (3 lb) roasting chicken
3 tablespoons oil
2 sprigs fresh curry leaves
1 large onion, finely chopped
2 cloves garlic, finely chopped
2 teaspoons finely chopped
   fresh ginger
3 teaspoons chilli powder
1 teaspoon ground turmeric

1 tablespoon ground coriander
1$^{1}/_{2}$ teaspoons ground cummin
$^{1}/_{2}$ teaspoon ground fennel
   salt to taste
2 medium ripe tomatoes,
   peeled and chopped
2 small sticks cinnamon
1 cup canned coconut milk

Joint chicken and cut large pieces across into halves. Heat oil in a heavy saucepan and gently fry curry leaves, onion, garlic and ginger until soft, stirring frequently. Stir in chilli powder and ground spices and fry for 2 minutes.

Add salt and tomatoes, stir to mix, then cover and simmer until tomatoes form a pulp. Add chicken pieces, turning them until coated with spice mixture. Add cinnamon sticks, cover and cook for 30 minutes, or until chicken is almost tender. Stir in coconut milk mixed with $^{1}/_{2}$ cup water and simmer, uncovered, for about 15 minutes more. Serve with rice and accompaniments.

duck vindaloo

Duck, being a rich and fatty meat, is improved by being cooked in a dish like Vindaloo with its high acid content to offset the richness.

serves 4-5

1 x 2.5 kg (5 lb) duck	2 teaspoons ground cummin
8 large dried red chillies	1 teaspoon Fragrant Garam
³/4 cup white wine vinegar	Masala (see p. 84)
4 cloves garlic, chopped	¹/2 teaspoon ground black pepper
1 tablespoon chopped	2 tablespoons oil
fresh ginger	salt to taste
1 tablespoon ground coriander	1 tablespoon brown sugar

Cut duck into joints. Remove and discard stalks and seeds from chillies and soak in vinegar for 10 minutes. Put chillies, vinegar, garlic and ginger into a blender and process until smooth. Transfer mixture to a large bowl and mix in ground spices. Add duck pieces and turn until well coated. Cover and leave for 2 hours, or refrigerate overnight.

Heat oil in a large non-aluminium saucepan and lightly fry duck pieces. Mix in salt and a little hot water with remaining marinade. Cover and simmer gently until duck is tender. Add a little more water if necessary during cooking. Stir in sugar when duck is cooked. Serve with rice.

devilled turkey

Giving leftovers a new image after the Christmas feast may not sound particularly Asian, but happens in many countries that have been converted to Christianity or colonised by the British. They therefore celebrate Christmas with the traditional fare. Try this spicy treatment of cold turkey.

serves 6

500 g (1 lb) cold, cooked turkey
2 teaspoons crushed garlic
1 teaspoon salt
1 teaspoon finely grated fresh ginger
1 tablespoon vinegar
1 tablespoon Worcestershire Sauce
1 or 2 tablespoons chilli sauce
2 tablespoons arrack or whisky
2 teaspoons prepared
   grain mustard
2 teaspoons sugar

1 teaspoon freshly ground pepper
2 tablespoons dripping from roast or ghee
2 large onions cut in thick slices
2 sprigs fresh curry leaves
   or about 20 dried leaves
strips of pandan leaf
1 stem lemon grass
2 cups turkey stock
4 whole cloves
   small stick of cinnamon
500 g (1 lb) potatoes, peeled and sliced

Cut turkey into joints or slices. Crush garlic with salt and mix with ginger, vinegar, Worcestershire Sauce, chilli sauce, arrack, mustard, sugar and pepper. Marinade turkey in mixture for 30 minutes.

Heat dripping in a heavy saucepan and fry onions, curry leaves, pandan leaf and lemon grass until onions are deep brown. Add marinated turkey, stock, cloves and cinnamon, cover and simmer for 15 minutes. Add potatoes, cover and cook until done. Serve hot.

chicken
in creamy sauce

A lightly spiced, creamy dish, sometimes called Butter Chicken.

serves 6

6 chicken thigh cutlets or 1 x
   1.5 kg (3 lb) roasting chicken
$^1/_4$ teaspoon saffron strands
2 teaspoons crushed garlic
1 tablespoon finely grated
   fresh ginger
1 tablespoon lemon juice
$^1/_2$ teaspoon chilli powder, optional
2 teaspoons paprika
1 teaspoon Kashmiri Garam
   Masala (see p. 82)
1 tablespoon ghee or butter

Sauce
1 tablespoon ghee or butter
2 teaspoons finely chopped garlic
1 onion, finely chopped
3 tablespoons tomato paste
$1^1/_2$ teaspoons salt
1 tablespoon sugar
1 tablespoon fine shreds of ginger
$^1/_2$ cup cream
1 teaspoon Kashmiri Garam
   Masala (see p. 82)
$^1/_4$ cup chopped fresh coriander

Cut chicken into joints. Toast saffron in dry pan for less than a minute, turn onto plate and crush with the back of a spoon. Dissolve in a tablespoon of hot water. Combine with remaining ingredients, except ghee, and rub over chicken. Set aside for an hour. Scrape off and reserve marinade. Fry chicken in 1 tablespoon ghee until lightly browned.

Sauce

In a heavy pan melt ghee or butter and cook garlic and onion until soft and translucent. Add reserved marinade, tomato paste dissolved in 1 cup water, salt, sugar and ginger shreds. Cover and simmer 10 minutes. Stir in cream. Add pieces of fried chicken, spoon sauce over, cover and cook until chicken is done, stirring occasionally. Sprinkle with Garam Masala and fresh coriander and serve with Indian bread or rice.

Note This dish is still delicious without saffron.

green
curry of duck with sataw nuts

Sataw nuts are the seeds of a giant bean, popular in southern Thailand. Their flavour and smell are definitely an acquired taste—only for adventurous curry buffs! In Malaysia and Indonesia they are called petai or peteh. Purchase them in cans or jars.

serves 6

1 x 2kg (4 lb) roasting duck
1 x 400 mL (14 fl oz) can
    coconut milk
3 tablespoons Thai Green
    Curry Paste (see p. 88)
6 kaffir lime leaves
2 tablespoons fish sauce
1/2 cup drained sataw nuts
    salt to taste
4 fresh green chillies, seeded
    and chopped
1/2 cup chopped fresh basil leaves

Cut duck into joints. Take $^3/_4$ cup of rich coconut milk and heat in a wok or heavy saucepan until thick and oily. Add Green Curry Paste and cook over low heat, stirring, 3 or 4 minutes or until fragrant and oily on surface. Add duck and remaining coconut milk mixed with 2 cups water.

Add lime leaves and fish sauce, stir well, cover and simmer for 1$^1/_2$ hours or until duck is almost tender. Add sataw nuts and salt to taste and simmer for a further 15 minutes. Just before serving stir in chillies and basil. Serve with rice.

hunan-style chicken

serves 4

6 large chicken thigh cutlets
1 teaspoon Szechwan
  peppercorns
1/2 teaspoon salt
2 tablespoons dark soy sauce
2 tablespoons dry sherry
2 teaspoons honey
3 tablespoons peanut oil

3 dried red chillies, cut in pieces
1/4 cup chopped spring onions
1 tablespoon finely
  chopped ginger
2 teaspoons finely chopped garlic
2 tablespoons Chinese vinegar
1 teaspoon chilli bean sauce
1 teaspoon sesame oil

Cut chicken thighs into bite-sized pieces, chopping through bone. Roast Szechwan peppercorns in a dry pan over low heat for a few minutes, shaking pan or stirring so they don't scorch. Grind to powder in mortar and pestle and sprinkle over chicken pieces with salt. Mix soy sauce, sherry and honey, pour over chicken and mix well.

Heat peanut oil in a wok and fry chillies, spring onions, ginger and garlic until fragrant, stirring constantly. Add chicken and stir-fry on high heat for 2 or 3 minutes, lower heat, cover and simmer until chicken is tender, about 7 minutes.

Combine vinegar, chilli bean sauce and sesame oil and pour over chicken. Toss a few times on high heat. Serve with steamed rice and vegetables.

Meat is used more as a condiment than as the main feature of a meal, since the precious land area cannot support cattle on a large scale. Pork is easy to raise and widely used except among Muslims. Mutton and beef usually need to be cooked long and slowly, an advantage when preparing curries, as long cooking not only tenderises meat but also blends and mellows spices.

lamb

koftas in saffron sauce

Typical of Kashmiri food, this curry has a rich red sauce with the fragrance of saffron.

serves 6

750 g (1¹/₂ lb) boneless lamb
1¹/₂ teaspoons Garam Masala
   (see p. 84)
1 teaspoon salt
3 tablespoons arrowroot
1 teaspoon turmeric
1 or 2 teaspoons chilli powder,
   to taste
2 tablespoons ghee or oil
1 medium onion, sliced finely

2 teaspoons finely chopped
   fresh ginger
1 small stick cinnamon
4 whole cloves
3 cardamom pods, bruised
2 teaspoons paprika
2 teaspoons tomato paste
¹/₄ teaspoon saffron strands
2 tablespoons finely chopped
   coriander leaves

Chop meat roughly into cubes and process in a food processor, a quarter at a time, until a smooth paste. Mix Garam Masala, salt and arrowroot with 2 tablespoons cold water until smooth. Add to meat. Form into ovals the size of an egg. Poach in a saucepan with 5 cm (2 inch) lightly salted boiling water, half the turmeric and chilli powder for 10 minutes.

Heat ghee or oil and fry onion, ginger and whole spices until onion is soft and golden. Stir in remaining turmeric and chilli powder with paprika and tomato paste. Add meat balls with some of their cooking liquid. Cover and simmer until tender—about 30 minutes. Lightly toast saffron strands in a dry pan, crush to powder and dissolve in 2 tablespoons boiling water. Stir in towards end of cooking and garnish with coriander leaves. Serve with rice and vegetables.

chilli
beef with snow peas

serves 4

375 g (12 oz) lean rump or
   fillet steak
1 teaspoon crushed garlic
1 tablespoon soy sauce
2 teaspoons chilli bean sauce
100 g ($3^1/_2$ oz) snow peas
6 spring onions

2 large red chillies
2 tablespoons peanut oil
$^1/_2$ cup beef stock
2 teaspoons cornflour
2 tablespoons Chinese wine or
   dry sherry
1 teaspoon sesame oil

Freeze beef just until firm enough to cut into paper-thin slices. Rub with a mixture of garlic, soy sauce and chilli bean sauce.

String snow peas and if large, cut in halves. Cut spring onions into bite-sized lengths. Seed and slice chillies.

Heat a wok, add oil and when oil is hot, add beef and stir-fry over high heat until meat is no longer pink. Add snow peas, onions, chillies and stir-fry a further minute. Add stock and bring to the boil, then stir in cornflour mixed with a tablespoon of cold water and stir until sauce clears and thickens. Add wine and sesame oil, give a quick toss through and serve at once with steamed rice.

spicy satay with peanut sauce

A popular dish throughout South East Asia. Ideal for barbecues.

serves 6

750 g (1¹/₂ lb) tender, lean pork
  or beef
1 large onion
2 cloves garlic
2 tablespoons light soy sauce
1 stem finely sliced lemon grass
  or grated rind of 1 lemon

3 teaspoons ground coriander
2 teaspoons ground cummin
1 teaspoon ground turmeric
¹/₂ teaspoon ground fennel
1 teaspoon salt
1 teaspoon sugar
Peanut Sauce (see p. 78)

Cut meat into small cubes. In food processor or blender purée onion, garlic, soy sauce and lemon grass or rind. Add remaining ingredients and blend again, then pour over meat, mix well to ensure all pieces are coated with marinade and leave for 1 hour or longer in refrigerator. Meanwhile, soak bamboo skewers in cold water so they will not burn readily.

Thread 5 or 6 pieces of meat on each skewer, leaving half bare. Wrap bare end in foil. Grill over barbecue or under a hot grill until brown. Serve with Peanut Sauce.

Note This recipe may also be prepared using chicken, preferably thigh fillets.

indonesian beef curry

One of my favourite curries, not only for its superb flavour, but for its easy preparation. A word of advice—although galangal is used in small amounts, its flavour is vital to the authenticity of rendang—Indonesia's most popular beef dish.

serves 8

1.5 kg (3 lb) lean stewing beef
3 large onions
4 large cloves garlic
1 tablespoon chopped
 fresh ginger
6 fresh red chillies or 1 tablespoon
 sambal ulek
1 stem fresh lemon grass, thinly
 sliced or grated rind of 1 lemon
2 teaspoons chopped greater
 galangal (laos)

1 teaspoon chopped lesser
 galangal (kencur) or $1/2$
 teaspoon dried ground kencur
1 tablespoon ground coriander
1 teaspoon ground cummin
1 teaspoon ground black pepper
$2^1/2$ cups canned coconut milk
1 tablespoon dried tamarind
 salt to taste
2 teaspoons palm or brown sugar

Cut beef into large cubes. Roughly chop onions and purée in a blender or food processor

with garlic, ginger, chillies or sambal ulek, lemon grass or rind, galangal and ground spices.

Put beef into a large saucepan with $1^1/2$ cups coconut milk mixed with $1^1/2$ cups water

and puréed mixture. Bring to the boil, stirring. Soak tamarind in $1/2$ cup hot water, squeeze to dissolve

pulp, and strain. Add tamarind liquid and about 2 teaspoons salt, reduce heat and simmer, uncovered,

until meat is tender and liquid has almost evaporated.

Add remaining coconut milk and the palm sugar, stirring constantly. Simmer again until

gravy is very thick and reduced to a small amount. Serve with steamed rice and a vegetable sayur

made as for Bean Sayur (see p. 60).

pork and liver curry

A specialty of Goa on the west coast of India. Reduce chillies if a hot curry is not to your taste.

serves 6-8

750 g (1¹/₂ lb) boneless pork
250 g (8 oz) calf's liver
12 large, dried red chillies
1 cup white wine vinegar
3 fresh green chillies,
   chopped roughly
2 tablespoons chopped
   fresh ginger
2 tablespoons chopped garlic

2 teaspoons ground coriander
2 teaspoons ground cummin
1 teaspoon ground turmeric
1 teaspoon ground cinnamon
¹/₂ teaspoon ground cloves
¹/₂ teaspoon ground black pepper
1¹/₂ teaspoons salt or to taste
1 tablespoon dried tamarind pulp
1 teaspoon brown sugar

Place pork in a saucepan with just enough lightly salted water to cover. Bring to boil and simmer gently for 5 minutes. Reserve pork stock and cut pork, including skin and fat, into large dice. Repeat with liver, but discard cooking liquid. Let liver cool and dice finely.

Discard stalks and seeds from dried chillies, soak chillies in vinegar for 10 minutes, then blend chillies, vinegar, green chillies, ginger and garlic to a purée. Add ground spices and salt.

In a non-aluminium saucepan put pork with stock, liver and spice mixture. Cover and simmer about 1 hour or until pork is tender. Dissolve tamarind in ¹/₂ cup hot water, strain and add with sugar to pan. Continue cooking, uncovered, until sauce is thick and dark. Serve with plain steamed rice.

burmese pork curry

Don't be daunted by the large amounts of garlic and ginger in this Burmese curry—they are essential to its wonderful flavour.

serves 8-10

2 kg (4 lb) pork
4 medium onions,
  chopped roughly
20 cloves garlic
1 cup peeled and roughly
  chopped fresh ginger
1 stem lemon grass or 3 strips
  lemon rind, finely chopped

2 teaspoons salt
2 tablespoons vinegar
2 teaspoons chilli powder
$3/4$ cup peanut oil
$1/4$ cup sesame oil
1 teaspoon ground turmeric

Cut pork into 2.5-cm (1-inch) cubes. Purée onions, garlic, ginger and lemon grass in a food processor or blender. Transfer to a stainless steel strainer set over a bowl.

With back of a spoon, push mixture to extract as much liquid as possible. Reserve solids and pour liquid into a large saucepan. Add pork, salt, vinegar, chilli and half the peanut oil. Bring to the boil, then reduce heat, cover and simmer gently for 1 to $1^1/2$ hours or until pork is almost tender, adding a little hot water if necessary.

In another large pan with heavy base, heat remaining peanut oil and sesame oil until very hot. Carefully add solids left in strainer—they will sputter. Stir in turmeric. Turn heat low and cook covered, but lift lid frequently to stir and scrape base of pan with a wooden spoon. If mixture fries too quickly and begins to stick before onions are transparent, stir in a little water from time to time. It is ready when ingredients have turned a rich red-brown colour, smell cooked, and oil has separated from the mass—about 25 minutes.

Add contents of first saucepan to cooked onion mixture, stir and cook, uncovered, until the oil separates once more and liquid has almost evaporated. Stir frequently to make sure mixture does not stick to base of pan. Serve with steamed rice and cooked vegetables or cucumber relish.

madras -style meat curry

The pungency of the chillies predominant in southern Indian curries is counteracted by plenty of rice—serving portions should comprise at least four parts rice to one part curry.

serves 6-8

1.5 kg (3 lb) lamb forequarter chops
  or other lamb cut
3 tablespoons oil
3 sprigs fresh curry leaves
2 large onions, finely chopped
3 cloves garlic, chopped
1 tablespoon finely chopped
  fresh ginger
1 teaspoon ground turmeric
1 tablespoon chilli powder,
  or to taste

1 tablespoon ground coriander
1 teaspoon ground cummin
1 small cinnamon stick
2 teaspoons salt or to taste
2 tablespoons lime or lemon juice
2 fresh green chillies, split halfway
  from tip
2 tablespoons desiccated coconut
$3/4$ cup canned coconut milk

Cut chops into pieces, incorporating bones for best flavour. Heat oil in a large, heavy-based saucepan and fry curry leaves until brown. Add onions, garlic and ginger and continue to fry, stirring frequently, until onions are soft and golden. Stir in turmeric and fry for a few seconds, then add chilli powder, coriander, cummin, and cinnamon stick, stir-frying for 1 minute more. Add salt and lime or lemon juice and cook, stirring, until liquid evaporates.

Add meat and turn pieces in spice mixture until thoroughly coated. Put in green chillies, reduce heat, cover and cook gently until meat is tender. There is no need to add any water.

Meanwhile toast coconut in a small, dry pan until golden brown, stirring occasionally. Process in blender or food processor until finely ground, adding $1/2$ cup water if necessary. Pour this into curry with coconut milk and $3/4$ cup water. Stir to mix and simmer, uncovered, until sauce thickens. Serve with rice and accompaniments.

pork vindaloo

(see p. 84)

serves 6-8

1 kg (2 lb) pork
6 large, dried red chillies
1 cup vinegar
2 teaspoons chopped fresh ginger
5 cloves garlic, chopped
2 teaspoons Garam Masala
  (see p. 84)

salt to taste
2 tablespoons dried tamarind pulp
2 tablespoons oil
2 medium onions, finely chopped
1 tablespoon brown sugar

Cut pork into cubes. Discard stalks and soak chillies in vinegar for 10 minutes, then purée chillies with ginger, garlic, Garam Masala and salt. Pour mixture over pork and stir to coat. Cover and marinate for 2 hours. Soak tamarind in $1^1/_2$ cups hot water, squeeze to dissolve pulp, strain through nylon sieve.

Heat oil in a non-aluminium saucepan and fry onions gently until golden, stirring frequently. Lift pork from marinade and fry over medium-high heat, tossing and stirring until pork changes colour. Add remaining marinade, tamarind and salt. Cover and simmer $1^1/_2$ hours or until pork is tender. Stir in brown sugar. Serve with rice.

masaman curry

Very popular in Thailand, this Muslim dish originated in India.

serves 6-8

1.5 kg (3 lb) blade or other
   stewing steak
6 cardamom pods
2^1/$_2$ cups canned coconut milk
4 tablespoons Masaman Curry
   Paste (see p. 87)
8 small new potatoes, scrubbed

10 small pickling onions, peeled
3 tablespoons fish sauce
3 tablespoons lime or lemon
   juice
1 tablespoon palm sugar
^{1}/$_2$ cup fresh basil leaves
^{1}/$_2$ cup whole roasted peanuts

Cut beef into large cubes and put into a pan with cardamom pods and 1^1/$_2$ cups of coconut milk diluted with an equal amount of water. Simmer until meat is almost tender.

Heat rest of undiluted coconut milk in a wok and reduce over medium heat, stirring, until thick and oily. Add Masaman Curry Paste and fry until fragrant. Add meat, potatoes, onions, fish sauce, lime or lemon juice and palm sugar. Cook until potatoes are done, adding some of stock from meat as required. Towards the end of cooking stir in basil leaves and peanuts. Serve with steamed rice.

jhal farezi

What do you do with a leftover lamb roast? Try this lightly spiced Indian dish.

serves 4

1 tablespoon ghee or butter
2 tablespoons oil
2 onions, sliced
1 teaspoon finely chopped garlic
1 teaspoon finely grated
 fresh ginger
1 teaspoon chilli powder or
 to taste
1 teaspoon turmeric
$^1/_2$ teaspoon ground black pepper
1 teaspoon Garam Masala
 (see p. 84)
 salt to taste
2 cups sliced cold meat
4-6 quartered or sliced cooked
 potatoes
 squeeze of lemon juice
 chopped fresh mint or coriander
 sliced tomato and cucumber

Heat ghee and oil in a frying pan or wok and fry onions on medium heat, stirring constantly, until they are deep brown. Add garlic and ginger and fry 1 minute longer, then add ground spices and salt and fry for a few seconds more. Add meat and potatoes and toss. Sprinkle with a few tablespoons of water, cover and heat through for 5 minutes.

Uncover and ensure that all liquid is evaporated. Sprinkle with lemon juice and herbs. Garnish with slices of tomato and cucumber and serve with steamed rice and a sweet chutney.

spicy spareribs

serves 6-8

2.5 kg (5 lb) lean, American-style
pork spareribs
4 large cloves garlic, peeled
1 teaspoon sugar
1 teaspoon salt
$1/2$ teaspoon five spice powder

$1/2$ teaspoon white pepper
$1/2$ teaspoon chilli powder
$1/4$ cup light soy sauce
2 tablespoons peanut oil
3 tablespoons tomato sauce
1 tablespoon honey

Ask butcher to cut ribs into short lengths and separate them into groups of 3 or 4 ribs.

Crush garlic with sugar and salt, mix with five spice powder, pepper, chilli powder and soy sauce. Pour over ribs, rubbing well. Marinate for 1 hour.

In a large, heavy frying pan heat peanut oil and brown ribs in batches. Add tomato sauce, honey and $1/2$ cup hot water stirred together until honey dissolves. Cover and simmer until tender, then spoon sauce over and cook uncovered until ribs are nicely glazed. (If you like, finish ribs over a barbecue.) Serve with steamed rice and a bottled sauce, such as sweet chilli sauce or plum sauce.

steamed layered pork

Long steaming ensures the pork is so tender it can be broken with chopsticks. Serve with plenty of steamed rice, because this dish is very rich.

serves 6-8

750 g (1¹/₂ lb) pork belly with layers
   of lean and fat
1 teaspoon chopped garlic
1 teaspoon sugar
2 teaspoons chilli bean sauce
¹/₃ cup dark soy sauce
2 tablespoons dry sherry
¹/₂ teaspoon five spice powder
3 tablespoons roasted
   rice powder (see p.91)

Have butcher remove skin and thick layer of fat next to it. Cut pork into large squares.

Crush garlic with sugar to a smooth purée and mix with chilli bean sauce, soy sauce, sherry and five spice powder.

Pour mixture over pork, mix well and marinate for 2 hours. Roll pork in roasted rice powder and place in a heatproof dish. Steam over boiling water on high heat for 2 hours, replacing water with more boiling water as it boils away. When done, fat should be transparent and pork very tender. Serve hot with rice and stir-fried or steamed vegetables.

In Asian cuisines you don't find the boiled-to-death vegetables responsible for generations of Anglo Saxons growing up with a determination not to eat them. In countries where much of the population is vegetarian, every dish sings with flavour. Judiciously spiced, some are dry while others have lots of sauce; some are mild while others would wake up the drowsiest tastebuds. All are delicious and healthy since none of the goodness is thrown out with the cooking water.

potato curry with tamarind

serves 4-6

750 g (1¹/₂ lb) potatoes
walnut-sized piece of dried
    tamarind pulp
3 teaspoons brown sugar
2 tablespoons ghee or oil
1 teaspoon black mustard seeds
1 teaspoon ground turmeric
1 teaspoon chilli powder or
    to taste
2 teaspoons ground coriander
1 teaspoon ground cummin
1 teaspoon salt or to taste
2 or 3 fresh chillies, sliced
2 tablespoons fresh grated or
    desiccated coconut

Peel potatoes and cut into cubes. Soak tamarind in ¹/₂ cup hot water and when cool enough, squeeze firmly to dissolve pulp, strain through a nylon or stainless steel strainer and discard seeds and fibres. Dissolve sugar in tamarind liquid.

Heat ghee or oil and fry mustard seeds, add turmeric, chilli powder, coriander and cummin and stir over low heat for 1 minute. Add potatoes and toss to coat with spices. Add salt and ¹/₄ cup water, cover with well-fitting lid and cook on very low heat for 15 minutes.

Stir in tamarind, chillies and coconut. Cover and cook until potatoes are tender. Serve with chapatis or rice.

bean sayur

Sayur, an Indonesian mildly spiced vegetable dish, is served with rice and a dry curry to round out a meal.

serves 6

2 tablespoons peanut oil
1 large onion, chopped
3 cloves garlic, finely chopped
3 fresh red chillies, seeded
   and chopped
1 teaspoon dried shrimp paste
1 stalk lemon grass, bruised
2 teaspoon ground coriander
1 teaspoon ground cummin

1 teaspoon finely chopped
   galangal
1 salam leaf or sprig of fresh
   curry leaves
3 cups chicken stock or water
1 cup canned coconut milk
500 g (1 lb) snake beans or green
   beans, sliced
salt to taste

Heat oil in a large saucepan and fry onion, garlic, chillies and shrimp paste. Add lemon grass, coriander, cummin and galangal and fry, stirring, for 1 minute. Add salam leaf, stock and coconut milk and bring to the boil, stirring. Add beans and salt to taste. Bring to the boil and simmer until beans are tender. Shredded cabbage, sliced zucchini or a mixture of vegetables can be used in the same way.

Note The salam leaf, used in Indonesian dishes, is sometimes available dried from Asian grocery stores. If you cannot obtain any, substitute fresh curry leaves.

spiced yellow pumpkin

serves 4

500 g (1 lb) yellow pumpkin
2 tablespoons oil
3 tablespoons toor dhal (see Note)
1 teaspoon black mustard seeds
10 curry leaves
1 clove garlic, finely chopped

2 teaspoons ground coriander
1 teaspoon ground cummin
1/2 teaspoon ground turmeric
1 teaspoon salt or to taste
3 tablespoons fresh, grated
   coconut or desiccated coconut

Peel and seed pumpkin, then cut into cubes. Heat oil in a saucepan and fry dhal, mustard seeds and curry leaves over low heat until mustard seeds pop and dhal is golden. Stir frequently. Add garlic and fry, stirring, for 1 minute, then stir in ground spices. Add pumpkin and salt and sufficient water to almost cover. Cover pan and simmer until pumpkin is half-cooked, then sprinkle with coconut and continue cooking until pumpkin is soft. Serve with rice.

Note Toor or tuvar dhal is also known as arhar dhal or red gram dhal. You can substitute split peas.

spicy fried cauliflower

serves 4-6

half a medium cauliflower
2 red chillies, optional
2 tablespoons oil
1¹/₂ teaspoons Whole Spice Mix
  (see p. 84)
2 teaspoons crushed garlic

2 teaspoons grated fresh ginger
1 teaspoon turmeric
1 teaspoon salt or to taste
3 tablespoons finely chopped
  coriander leaves

Break cauliflower into florets and slice each thickly. Slice chillies. Heat oil in a heavy-based saucepan and fry Whole Spice Mix (Panch Phora), stirring constantly, until mustard seeds pop. Add garlic, ginger and chillies, stir and fry for a few seconds, then add turmeric, salt and cauliflower. Toss until cauliflower is coated with spices. Add 2 tablespoons water and cover pan immediately to keep in steam.

Cook covered, over medium heat, shaking pan from time to time for about 8 minutes. Add 1 tablespoon extra water if necessary. Cauliflower should be tender but still crisp. Mix in chopped coriander and serve with rice or Chapatis (see p. 77).

eggplant and potato curry

serves 6

500 g (1 lb) eggplant
2 large potatoes
2 large, ripe tomatoes
3 tablespoons mustard oil
   or vegetable oil
2 medium onions, finely chopped
2 teaspoons finely chopped ginger
1 clove garlic, crushed

1 teaspoon cummin seeds,
   crushed
$1/2$ teaspoon ground turmeric
2 fresh green chillies, seeded and
   finely sliced
salt to taste
1 teaspoon brown sugar

Wash eggplant and cut into small cubes. Peel and dice potatoes; blanch, peel and chop tomatoes. Heat oil in a heavy, deep frying pan until it begins to smoke. Toss in potato cubes and fry until golden, then remove with slotted spoon and set aside. Add eggplant cubes and fry, stirring, until lightly browned. Remove from pan. Add a little more oil if necessary, as eggplant soaks it up.

Add onion and fry over low heat, stirring frequently, until soft and golden. Stir in ginger, garlic, cummin and turmeric and fry for 1 minute more. Add chillies, tomatoes and salt, then stir in reserved potatoes and eggplant. Cover and cook over low heat, adding $1/2$ cup water if necessary. Stir in sugar and cook, uncovered, until liquid evaporates. Serve with rice or Chapatis (see p. 77).

ma
po dou fu

Quite a famous dish, this is a perfect example of how to put zip into an ingredient as bland as bean curd.

serves 4

3 pieces dried wood fungus
500 g (1 lb) firm bean curd
3 tablespoons peanut oil
2 tablespoons finely chopped
    fresh ginger
2 teaspoons finely chopped garlic
1/3 cup chopped spring onion
125 g (4 oz) minced pork

1 cup chicken or pork stock
1 teaspoon chilli bean sauce,
    or to taste
1 tablespoon ground bean sauce
2 tablespoons tomato ketchup
2 teaspoons cornflour
2 teaspoons oriental sesame oil
    red chilli, optional

Soak wood fungus in cold water for 10 minutes until swollen, cut into bite-sized pieces, discarding any woody portions. Dice bean curd, drop into boiling water and let water return to boil for a few minutes to heat bean curd through, then drain in a colander.

Heat oil in a wok and fry ginger, garlic and spring onion over medium heat, stirring, until fragrant. Add pork and stir-fry, pressing it against side of wok until it is no longer pink. Mix stock, chilli bean sauce, ground bean sauce and tomato ketchup, pour into wok and simmer for 5 minutes. Mix cornflour with a tablespoon of cold water and stir into sauce until it boils and thickens.

Gently stir in drained bean curd, wood fungus and sesame oil, heat through and serve on steamed rice. Garnish with red chilli if liked.

spicy mashed potatoes

serves 4-6

750 g (1¹/₂ lb) potatoes
1 tablespoon ghee or oil
1 teaspoon black mustard seeds
1 onion, finely chopped
1 or 2 fresh chillies, sliced
1 teaspoon Garam Masala
(see p. 84)

¹/₂ teaspoon ground turmeric
1 teaspoon salt or to taste
¹/₄ teaspoon chilli powder
2 tablespoons lemon juice
¹/₄ cup chopped fresh mint
or coriander

Boil potatoes in skins, peel while still hot and mash smoothly. Heat ghee and fry mustard seeds until they pop. Add onion and fresh chillies and fry until onion is soft and golden. Stir in Garam Masala, turmeric, salt and chilli powder and stir well for a few seconds, then add lemon juice and potatoes, mixing flavours in thoroughly and heating through. Serve sprinkled with fresh mint or coriander.

spicy
diced vegetables

serves 4

2 medium carrots
2 large potatoes
2 firm, ripe tomatoes
250 g (8 oz) snake beans or
    green beans
2 tablespoons mustard oil or
    vegetable oil
2 teaspoons black mustard seeds
2 onions, chopped finely

1 clove garlic, chopped
1 teaspoon finely chopped
    fresh ginger
1 teaspoon ground coriander
1 teaspoon ground cummin
$^{1}/_{2}$ teaspoon chilli powder
    salt to taste
$^{1}/_{2}$ teaspoon Garam Masala
    (see p. 84)

Peel carrots, potatoes and tomatoes and cut into dice. Trim beans and cut into small pieces—about the same size as diced vegetables.

Heat oil in a heavy-based saucepan and fry mustard seeds until they pop. Add onions, garlic and ginger and fry, stirring frequently, until onion is golden. Stir in coriander, cummin and chilli powder and fry for a few seconds, then toss in vegetables until coated with spices and oil. Add salt to taste. Add 3 tablespoons water, cover and cook 15 minutes, or until vegetables are tender. Stir gently every 5 minutes and add a little more water if necessary. Sprinkle with Garam Masala just before end of cooking. Serve with rice or Chapatis (see p. 77).

thai
eggplant curry

serves 4

500 g (1 lb) eggplant
$^1/_2$ cup oil for deep-frying
2 tablespoons Pepper and
    Coriander Paste (see p. 86)
    or Thai Green Curry Paste
    (see p. 88)
1 cup canned coconut milk
4 kaffir lime leaves
1-2 tablespoons fish sauce
1 tablespoon palm sugar

Wash and dry eggplants but do not peel. If using slender eggplants, cut into slices, otherwise cut into large cubes. Deep-fry in hot oil until browned, remove and drain on paper towels.

In 1 tablespoon oil fry Pepper and Coriander Paste or Thai Green Curry Paste over low heat, stirring, until fragrant. Add coconut milk and 1 cup water, lime leaves, fish sauce and palm sugar. Stir and simmer for 5 minutes, then add eggplant and simmer for 10 minutes longer or until eggplant is tender. Serve with rice.

lentil and vegetable soup

serves 6

1 cup split peas or red lentils
1 tablespoon dried tamarind pulp
2 tablespoons oil
1 tablespoon ground coriander
2 teaspoons ground cummin
1½ teaspoons ground black pepper
½ teaspoon ground turmeric
⅛ teaspoon asafoetida

3 cups mixed vegetables
   (zucchini, eggplant, beans,
   pumpkin, potatoes),
   diced small
2 fresh green chillies, seeded
   and sliced
   salt to taste
½ teaspoon black mustard seeds
1 small onion, finely sliced

Wash split peas or lentils well. (If using peas soak for at least 2 hours or overnight. Lentils do not need soaking.) Drain and place in saucepan with 6 cups water and simmer until soft. Soak tamarind pulp in 1 cup hot water and squeeze until pulp is dissolved. Strain, discarding seeds and fibres. Add to lentils.

In a heavy saucepan heat 2 teaspoons of oil and fry ground spices and asafoetida over low heat, stirring, for a few seconds. Add lentil mixture, vegetables and chillies and simmer until vegetables are cooked. Add salt to taste.

Heat remaining oil in a small, heavy frying pan and fry mustard seeds and onion until seeds pop and onion is brown. Stir frequently so onion does not burn. Stir into soup; simmer a few minutes longer and serve as a soup, or a one-dish meal with steamed rice.

The staple food of Asia is rice. It is the foundation on which meals are built and while meat, fish, poultry or vegetables are necessary to enliven the blandness of plain rice they are of secondary importance. Sometimes chapatis and other breads take the place of rice. Remember that there should be three or four times as much rice or bread to offset the spiciness of other dishes. The starch helps cushion the effect of strong spices and rich gravy.

To cook rice perfectly by the absorption method, first wash and drain the rice well. For each cup of rice allow $1\frac{1}{2}$ cups of cold water. Put rice and water into a saucepan with a well-fitting lid, add salt or not as you prefer, and bring to the boil. Cover tightly with lid, turn heat very low and cook for 15 minutes without lifting lid. Remove from heat and let it sit for a further 5 minutes. Each cup of raw rice should yield three or four servings.

assorted
raitas (yoghurt coolers)

Raitas may be made with many vegetables or herbs stirred into seasoned yoghurt. Coconut is optional. Use diced, cooked or canned beetroot; finely chopped or blended mint leaves; or diced seedless cucumbers sprinkled with salt and left for 20 minutes to draw out excess liquid (rinse and drain before stirring through yoghurt mixture).

serves 6

4 ripe bananas
lime or lemon juice
1 teaspoon cummin seeds
1 cup plain yoghurt
$^1/_4$ cup freshly grated or desiccated coconut
salt to taste
2 teaspoons sugar

Slice bananas, sprinkle well with lime juice and set aside. Toast cummin seeds in a small, dry pan, stirring constantly until browned, then crush. Put yoghurt in a bowl and combine with remaining ingredients. (Desiccated coconut should be sprinkled with about 2 tablespoons water and tossed with fingers until thoroughly moistened.) Fold banana slices into yoghurt mixture. Cover and chill until ready to serve as an accompaniment to rice and curry.

paratha

Rich, flaky and deliciously flavoured with ghee, the paratha is a popular Indian bread.

makes 16

2 cups fine wholemeal flour
2 cups plain flour
1¹/₂ teaspoons salt
8 tablespoons ghee
extra ghee for cooking

Sieve flours and salt into a mixing bowl and rub in 2 tablespoons of ghee. Add 1¹/₂ cups lukewarm water, mix and knead dough for at least 10 minutes (the more it is kneaded, the lighter the bread will be). Form dough into a ball, cover with clear plastic wrap and set aside for 1 hour.

Divide dough into 16 equal portions and roll each into a smooth ball. Melt remaining ghee and allow to cool slightly. Roll out each ball of dough on a lightly floured board into a very thin circle. Put 2 teaspoons of ghee in centre of each and spread lightly by hand. With a knife make a cut from centre of circle to outer edge. Starting at cut edge, roll dough closely into a cone shape. Pick up, press apex and base of cone towards each other and flatten slightly. You will now have a small roughly circular lump of dough again. Lightly flour board and roll out dough very gently, not as thinly as the first time. Take care not to press too hard or air will come out at edges. Parathas should be as round as possible.

Cook on a hot griddle or in a heavy pan liberally greased with extra ghee, turning parathas and spreading with more ghee, until golden brown. Serve hot.

Note When rolling out chapatis, puris and parathas, please remember to keep them separate. If allowed to touch they will stick together. If space dictates they have to be stacked, sprinkle each with flour and lay a square of greaseproof paper over. Make sure paper is large enough to cover the whole circle of dough, otherwise the unprotected ends will attach themselves to the next circle and spoil the nice round shape.

Chapatis

In India this unleavened wholemeal bread is cooked on a griddle called a tawa.
A heavy-based frying pan or griddle plate can be used instead.

makes 18-20

3 cups atta or roti flour
salt to taste
1 tablespoon ghee
1 cup lukewarm water

Put flour into a mixing bowl. Mix in salt, then rub in ghee. Add water all at once and mix to a firm but not stiff dough. Knead dough for about 10 minutes—longer kneading will give lighter bread. (You can also make dough in a food processor to reduce kneading time.) Shape dough into a ball, cover with clear plastic wrap and let stand for at least 1 hour.

Form dough into walnut-sized balls. Roll out each one on a lightly floured board to a very thin circle. Once all are rolled, heat a griddle plate or frying pan and cook chapatis, starting with those that were rolled first (resting time makes the chapatis lighter). Place chapati on griddle and leave for about 1 minute. Turn and cook other side for a further minute, pressing lightly around edges with a folded tea towel. This encourages bubbles to form. As each one is cooked, wrap immediately in a clean, dry tea towel until all are ready.

puris

Have the oil moderately hot for this Indian deep-fried wholemeal bread so it fries without absorbing too much oil and becoming greasy.

makes 24

Ingredients as for Chapatis

Proceed as above but make discs smaller, about the size of a small saucer. When all of dough is rolled into rounds, pour a depth of about 2.5 cm (1 inch) oil into a deep frying pan. Heat oil until a faint haze rises from surface. Fry puris one at a time over moderate heat, spooning hot oil continually over surface of each, as this makes them puff and swell. Turn over and fry other side. When pale golden brown on both sides, remove and drain on paper towels. Serve immediately with curries.

peanut sauce

This sauce base is diluted with coconut milk or water to give a pouring consistency and can be combined with lightly steamed vegetables to make that Indonesian speciality Gado Gado. In its undiluted it form makes a wonderful spread for savoury crackers or tiny, bite-sized sandwiches as a cocktail savoury.

makes about
2 1/2 cups

1/2 cup peanut oil
1 tablespoon dried garlic flakes
3 or 4 large, dried red chillies
3 tablespoons crisp fried onions
1 teaspoon dried shrimp paste
2 tablespoons dark soy sauce

2 tablespoons strained lime juice
1 x 375 g (12 oz) jar crunchy
   peanut butter
2 tablespoons coarse sugar
   (raw sugar or coffee crystals)

Heat oil and fry garlic flakes on gentle heat until pale gold, remove immediately with a slotted spoon or lower into oil on a fine mesh strainer so you can lift them out as soon as they turn pale gold. Drain on absorbent paper.

Fry chillies quite slowly until puffed, crisp and quite dark in colour. Drain and cool, then discard stems and crumble or chop chillies into small pieces. If using ready-fried onions, simply crush into bits.

In same oil cook shrimp paste, crushing with back of spoon. Add soy sauce and lime juice and stir to dissolve. Remove from heat. Stir in peanut butter and allow to cool completely before mixing in fried garlic, onions, chillies and sugar. Store in a wide-mouthed jar in refrigerator. Heat 1/2 cup of sauce base and add about 1/2 cup diluted coconut milk or water to give a pouring consistency.

sweet and hot garlic chilli sauce

makes about
4 cups

250 g (8 oz) fresh red chillies
750 g (1½ lb) white sugar
1 x 750 mL (26 fl oz) bottle
white vinegar
375 g (12 oz) sultanas
10-15 cloves garlic, peeled
2 tablespoons finely grated
fresh ginger
3 teaspoons salt or to taste

Wear rubber gloves when handling chillies. Cut off and discard stems and, if preferred, cut chillies down centre and scrape out seeds.

In a non-aluminium saucepan combine all ingredients and simmer until chillies, garlic and sultanas are very soft. Cool and purée in food processor or push through a sieve. Pour into sterilised bottles and seal.

fresh coriander and coconut chutney

serves 6

1 bunch fresh coriander
¼ cup desiccated coconut
1 clove garlic, chopped
1 fresh green chilli, seeded
1 teaspoon Garam Masala
(see p. 84)
salt to taste
2 tablespoons lime or lemon juice

Wash coriander and put into a blender or food processor with other ingredients. Process until smooth, adding 3 tablespoons or so of water, but don't allow the mixture to become too wet.

Transfer to a small bowl, cover and chill. Serve as an accompaniment to curries and rice.

The key to the best flavours is to know what should go into spice mixtures and ensure that they do. Correctly stored away from heat and light in a tightly stoppered jar, ground spices keep their fragrance for months.

Curry pastes also keep well if stored in a glass jar in the refrigerator and if a clean, dry spoon is used to remove the required quantity, or divide curry pastes into meal-sized portions, wrap and freeze, not forgetting to label them carefully. Once you have made them it is possible to produce Asian meals in very little time. The results are vastly different from using commercial mixtures.

ceylon curry powder

Asian spice stores sell Ceylon curry powder—it differs from other spice mixtures in that the spices are first roasted until dark brown. You can make your own curry powder, however, with the following recipe.

makes about
1¹/₂ cups

1 cup coriander seeds
¹/₂ cup cummin seeds
1 tablespoon fennel seeds
1 teaspoon fenugreek seeds
1 x 5-cm (2-inch) cinnamon stick
1 teaspoon whole cloves

1 teaspoon cardamom seeds
2 tablespoons dried curry leaves
2 teaspoons chilli powder,
    optional
2 tablespoons ground rice,
    optional

Roast separately coriander, cummin, fennel and fenugreek in a dry pan over low heat, stirring constantly, until each one turns a fairly dark brown. Do not let them burn. Put into a blender container with cinnamon stick broken into pieces, cloves, cardamom and curry leaves. Blend on high speed until finely powdered. Mix with chilli powder and ground rice if used. Store in an airtight jar.

kashmiri garam masala

2 tablespoons cummin seeds
2 tablespoons fennel seeds
1 tablespoon cardamom seeds
    (measure after removing pods)
1 teaspoon kalonji (nigella) seeds
1 teaspoon whole black
    peppercorns
1 x 5-cm (2-inch) cinnamon stick
¹/₂ teaspoon whole cloves
1 nutmeg, grated

Roast spices, except nutmeg, separately in a small, heavy-based frying pan. As each batch begins to give out a fragrant aroma, remove from pan and leave to cool. Combine in blender and grind to a fine powder, then add grated nutmeg. Store in an airtight jar in a cool, dry, dark place.

whole
spice mix (panch phora)

makes about
1/2 cup

2 tablespoons black
mustard seeds
2 tablespoons cummin seeds
2 tablespoons kalonji
(nigella) seeds
1 tablespoon fenugreek seeds
1 tablespoon fennel seeds

Mix all ingredients and put into a jar with airtight lid.

Shake before use to ensure seeds are evenly distributed.

garam
masala

Buy good quality whole spices and, once ground, store the mixtures in airtight jars in a cool, dry and dark cupboard. This will help to preserve the flavour and fragrance.

makes about
3/4 cup

4 tablespoons coriander seeds
2 tablespoons cummin seeds
1 tablespoon whole
black peppercorns
2 teaspoons cardamom seeds
(measure after roasting and
removing from pods)
4 x 7.5-cm (3-inch) cinnamon sticks
1 teaspoon whole cloves
1 whole nutmeg

Roast each whole spice separately, except for nutmeg, in a small, heavy-based pan. Turn each one out onto a plate to cool as soon as it smells fragrant. Peel and discard pods from roasted cardamoms, using only seeds. Grind all ingredients in a blender to a fine powder. Finely grate nutmeg and mix in. Store in glass jar with airtight lid.

fragrant
garam masala

makes about
1/4 cup

3 x 7.5-cm (3-inch) cinnamon sticks
2 teaspoons cardamom seeds
(measure after removing pods)
1 teaspoon whole cloves
1 teaspoon blades of mace

Roast spices separately in a small, heavy-based pan as in the recipe for Garam Masala (see above). When cool, grind in a blender or with a mortar and pestle. Store in an airtight jar.

pepper
and coriander paste

Pepper and Coriander Paste is one of the most useful items to have in the refrigerator.
It keeps very well, but if you don't want to use it as fast as I do, it may be wise to add
1 teaspoon citric acid dissolved in a tablespoon or so of hot water.

makes about
1 cup

1 tablespoon chopped garlic
2 teaspoons salt
2 tablespoons whole
    black peppercorns
2 cups coarsely chopped fresh
    coriander, including roots
2 tablespoons lemon juice

Crush garlic with salt to a smooth paste. Roast peppercorns in a dry pan for 1 or 2 minutes,

then coarsely crush in a mortar and pestle. Finely chop coriander roots, leaves and stems. Mix

all ingredients.

You can make this paste in a blender, but reduce black peppercorns to 1 tablespoon, as they

are hotter when more finely ground. Store in an airtight jar in the refrigerator.

Note Some of the ways I use this paste include marinating chicken fillets with a good thick coating

of it for 1 hour, then cooking them on the barbecue. Or, if I want a quick green chutney and don't have

any fresh herbs on hand, stir a spoonful of the paste into a cup of natural yoghurt. If you run out of

Thai Green Curry Paste never hesitate to use Pepper and Coriander Paste instead.

masaman curry paste

Masaman curry is spicy but sweet. Popular in Thailand, it has its origins in India.
This paste is useful to save preparation time.

makes about
1 cup

10 large, dried red chillies
2 tablespoons oil
2 large onions, finely chopped
1 tablespoon chopped garlic
2 teaspoons dried shrimp paste
1 tablespoon chopped greater
  galangal
2 teaspoons chopped krachai
2 stems lemon grass, finely sliced

2 tablespoons ground coriander
1 tablespoon ground cummin
2 teaspoons ground fennel
1 teaspoon ground cinnamon
1 teaspoon ground cardamom
1 teaspoon ground mace
  or nutmeg
1/2 teaspoon ground cloves

Wearing gloves, snip off stems of chillies and shake out the seeds (or leave them in if you
like hot curries). Soak in boiling water for 10 minutes.

Heat oil and fry onions and garlic over gentle heat until golden. Add shrimp paste and fry
a little longer. Allow to cool.

In an electric blender purée fried mixture with soaked chillies and a little of the soaking
water, galangal, krachai and lemon grass.

Roast coriander, cummin and fennel in a dry pan, stirring frequently—do not let them burn.
When fragrant turn out onto a plate and cool. Combine with cinnamon, cardamom, mace or nutmeg
and cloves and stir into puréed ingredients. Bottle in an airtight jar and store in refrigerator for up to
4 weeks.

thai
red curry paste

Red and green curry pastes are two of the basics of Thai cooking. Store any paste not used immediately in a clean, dry glass jar in the refrigerator, or divide into convenient portions and freeze.

makes about
1 cup

4-6 dried red chillies
2 small brown onions, chopped
1 teaspoon black peppercorns
2 teaspoons ground cummin
1 tablespoon ground coriander
1 teaspoon salt
1 stem lemon grass, finely sliced
  or 2 teaspoons chopped
  lemon rind

2 tablespoons chopped fresh
  coriander, including root
2 teaspoons chopped galangal
  in brine
1 tablespoon chopped garlic
2 teaspoons dried shrimp paste
1 teaspoon turmeric
2 teaspoons paprika

Remove stems from chillies (if you want curry to be as hot as it is in Thailand, leave seeds in). Break chillies into pieces, soak in just enough water to cover for 10 minutes, then place in an electric blender with remaining ingredients. Purée, stopping frequently to push ingredients down with a spatula. You might need to add extra water to assist with blending.

thai
green curry paste

makes about
1 cup

4 large or 8 small green chillies
1 medium onion, chopped
1 tablespoon chopped garlic
1/2 cup chopped fresh coriander,
  including roots, stems
  and leaves
1/4 cup finely sliced lemon grass,
  or thinly peeled rind of 1 lemon

1 tablespoon chopped galangal,
  fresh or bottled
2 teaspoons ground coriander
1 teaspoon ground cummin
1 teaspoon black peppercorns
1 teaspoon ground turmeric
1 teaspoon dried shrimp paste

With rubber gloves, remove stems and roughly chop chillies. Put into an electric blender with remaining ingredients and purée. Add a little water if necessary to help blending.

glossary

These ingredients are available in Asian food stores, but most of them are also sold in supermarkets.

Asafoetida
The dried, resinous gum of a plant that grows in Afghanistan and Iran. Widely used in Indian lentil dishes, for flavour and anti-flatulent effect. Sold in Indian stores. No substitute.

Atta
Fine wholemeal flour favoured for making chapatis and flat breads. Sold in Indian and some health food stores. Substitute fine wholemeal mixed with plain white flour.

Bean sauce
There are two kinds sold in glass jars: one is smooth, labelled 'refined bean sauce'; the other contains pieces of soy bean. Substitute dark soy sauce.

Cardamom
Strongly fragrant seed pods of a plant of the ginger family, there are two kinds: large black pods or small green pods. Use the latter, bruised slightly to release fragrance. For ground cardamom, open pods and pound the small brown or black seeds inside with a mortar and pestle.

Chillies
Wear gloves when chopping, slicing or removing seeds of fresh chillies, as the volatile oils can cause much discomfort. Small chillies are the hottest. It is possible to buy fresh, chopped chillies in jars or substitute sambal ulek (oelek), which is a mixture of fresh chillies and salt, or Tabasco Pepper Sauce (use 1 teaspoon for each hot chilli). Where large, dried chillies are called for, use the Asian variety, not the mild Californian or Mexican kind. Chilli powder also varies in intensity, depending on the chillies it is made from.

Chilli Bean Sauce
A super hot mixture of salted soy beans and chillies in oil. Use sparingly.

Chinese vinegar
There are various kinds, all of them milder than western wine or cider vinegars, so dilute if substituting one for the other.

Cinnamon
Often the thick, woody bark of cassia, which has a strong flavour and dark colour, is sold as cinnamon. True cinnamon is pale brown and much thinner, almost like parchment, and comprises 4 or 5 layers of fine bark rolled into quills.

Cloves
The dried flower buds of a native South-east Asian tree, which contain a powerful antiseptic oil that keeps meats from putrefying—used for over 2000 years as a preservative as well as a flavouring. Use sparingly as it can overpower other flavours. Nearest substitute is allspice.

Coconut milk
Readily available but some brands of canned coconut milk are thick and rich, others very thin. Mix the former with at least an equal amount of water, use the latter undiluted.

Coriander
The finely ground, dried seeds are used in almost every curry. Sometimes they are roasted first to subtly emphasize the flavour. The fresh herb is also used and in Thailand the herb's root is an important flavour in curry pastes. Use the leaves as garnish and for extra flavour.

Cummin
Sold as whole seeds or ground, this spice has a lemony fragrance and is a major component of curries.

Curry leaves
A compound leaf with great flavour. Some nurseries and Asian stores now sell the plant. They will grow in a temperate climate if sheltered from frosts. Fresh leaves are preferable to dried.

Fennel seeds
Larger and lighter coloured than cummin, with a licorice flavour.

Fenugreek seeds
One of the essential ingredients in curry powder, these pale beige seeds have a bitter undertone. Use in small quantities.

Five spice powder
Ground star anise, fennel, cinnamon, cloves and Szechwan pepper.

Galangal
There are two species of galangal—greater and lesser. Greater galangal is similar in size and appearance to ginger. Galangal is sold in jars or frozen, dried or powdered, the latter being known as laos powder. Laos, lengkuas, kha are some of its local names. Some Asian food stores may even sell it fresh. Lesser galangal is sold dried and ground it is most likely to be labelled its Indonesian name 'kencur' (kentjur).

Ghee
Clarified butter sold in tins, it can be heated to a high temperature because it has no milk solids that will burn. If unobtainable, make it by heating unsalted butter in a heavy-based pan and simmer for about 1 hour to evaporate water content, letting milk solids settle. Strain it through fine cheese cloth. Ghee keeps without refrigeration and gives a wonderful flavour to food.

Ginger
Fresh ginger root is sold at most greengrocers. Dried ground ginger should not be substituted.

Kaffir lime leaves
Essential ingredient available fresh, frozen or dried.

Kalonji seeds (nigella)
Sold mostly in Indian food stores, the small black seeds have a little point on one end. It has a lovely nutty flavour and will keep indefinitely in an airtight jar. An essential part of Indian whole spice mix, panch phora. No substitute.

Krachai
A rhizome used in Thai cooking. Sold in jars in a brine solution, either whole (it looks like small carrots) or cut in strips. May also be labelled 'kachai'.

Palm sugar
Obtained from various tropical palms, it has a distinctive flavour but can be substituted by brown sugar.

Rice powder, roasted
This gives a distinctive flavour to certain dishes and should not be omitted. It is sold in small packets in some Asian shops, particularly those which carry Thai and Vietnamese ingredients. If unavailable you can make it by roasting rice grains over low heat in a heavy pan for about 15 minutes until a deep golden brown. Stir constantly so they don't burn. Cool, then grind to powder in blender.

Saffron
Try to get true saffron because there are imitations, but nothing else has the same flavour. Expensive, but very little is needed. Keeps well if stored airtight. Buy the strands that are the dried stigmas of the autumn crocus, or tiny packets of powder. Distrust cheap saffron—there is no such thing.

Sesame oil
The sesame oil used in Eastern recipes is oriental sesame oil made from toasted sesame seeds. It is dark golden in colour and very different in flavour from light sesame oil sold in health food stores. It is usually used as a flavouring at the end of cooking. Just a few drops are sufficient.

Shrimp paste
Made from dried shrimp, this is powerful but if used in tiny quantities makes a great difference in flavour. Sold in jars or blocks. Keeps indefinitely.

Sweet chilli sauce
Looks like tomato ketchup. There are many to choose from, all varying in heat. Some contain garlic and ginger.

Szechwan pepper
Small dried berries that are not hot in the conventional sense, but leave a numbing sensation on the tongue. Only the brown husks provide flavour. Roast over a low heat to make them aromatic and crush to powder.

Tamarind
The fruit of a tropical tree, tamarind imparts acidity to many dishes. It is sold dried (the truest flavour), puréed and instant. Some puréed or instant tamarind products can be too acid or salty. Check the product's strength before adding and adjust quantity accordingly.

Turmeric
A rhizome of the ginger family with bright yellow flesh under a brown skin. Mostly available dried and ground, it is a component in commercial curry blends.

index